MW01620274
This Yael book belongs to:
..............................................

# Yael's Pesach Dance

This book is dedicated in loving memory to our unforgettable
Mother, Grandmother and Great-Grandmother

**Mrs. Genendl** bas Rav Shlomo **Berkowitz**, *zt"l*

Whose attributes, bravery, contentment, diligence, devotion, exertions, frugality, gentleness, humaneness, love, intelligence, perseverance, quiet demeanor, righteousness, simplicity, sincerity, tenacity, uniqueness, work ethic and wisdom continue to inspire, motivate and energize our lives as we endeavor to walk in her balanced path of דרך הממוצע.

Avrohom Pinchas and Mindy Berkowitz,
children and grandchildren, עמו"ש

Published by Lite Girl, Inc.

www.bealitegirl.com





ISBN: 978-1-60763-179-8
Library of Congress Cataloging number: 1-617005720

*Manufactured in China*

Distributed by: The Judaica Press, Inc.
www.judaicapress.com | 800.972.6201

Summary: In this book, the first of the Yael Yom Tov heritage series, Yael wonders what's so special about Pesach, which requires so much cleaning and preparation. Join Yael as she learns about our beautiful heritage, which began with Pesach long ago and will take us right until the ultimate redemption.

Credits:
Illustrations: Steve Pileggi/Blue Lion Designs
Cover design: 3G Design
Editor: Tzippy Caton
Audio CD produced and edited by Reuven A. Stone
Song recorded at Harlyn Studios (Celebration, FL)
Vocals recorded at Uptop Studios (Monsey, NY)
and engineered by Hillel Kapnick

Yael came home from school one day and found Mommy unpacking a new broom, a mop and a bunch of new closet hangers. "Pesach is coming!" said Mommy. "Tonight we're cleaning my room! It's time to start getting ready."

Every day after that, Mommy was filled with a new "busy-ness."
She wrote lists and lists and lists!
There was even a special Pesach song Mommy liked to sing ...
"Pesach is coming — hooray, hooray!"

Clean the bedrooms!
Clean the closets!
Clean the living room!
Clean the kitchen!
Call the carpet cleaner!
Send clothes to the cleaners!
Buy new shoes and new
Pesach clothes!

“What’s so ‘hooray’ about Pesach coming?” Yael asked one day.
“It seems like so much work!”

"The work is worth it," Mommy said as she did a little dance with the mop.
"Very soon, on the night of our Seder, we will sit like Kings and Queens!"

Yael was curious to see what Savta had to say.
"My Mommy is cleaning and cleaning, all day!" Yael said one afternoon during a visit to her grandmother.
Savta's eyes twinkled.
"Yes, very soon everything will sparkle and shine.
I love this time of year!"
"Do you love Pesach cleaning, too?" Yael wanted to know.
"I do!" Savta said happily.

"Do you sing while you clean?"

"I do that too!" Savta chuckled.

"Do you dance while you mop?"

"I do love to dance, Yael dear! The vacuum cleaner and I can twirl for hours!"

"But I don't understand," Yael sighed. "What makes Pesach so exciting?"

Savta sat on the sofa and patted the spot next to her. Yael snuggled close.

"Let me tell you a story."

"A long time ago," Savta began, "there was a very bad king. His name was Pharaoh. He made all the Jewish families very sad. In his kingdom, the Jewish people were slaves and had to work very hard."

Yael frowned. "That was a sad story." She didn't like sad stories.

“But then,” Savta exclaimed, “a wonderful thing happened! Hashem saw how sad the Jewish people were and He said, ‘It’s time to punish this terrible king! It’s time for the Jews to be happy!’ ”

"Hashem made many wonderful miracles that Abba will tell you about at the Seder. And then, Hashem did the best thing of all. Hashem chose the Jewish people to be special. He took us away from that terrible Egyptian land. He miraculously saved us by splitting the Red Sea so we could escape from Pharaoh's army, who were chasing us!"

"He drowned the army after we safely crossed, so we would never have to be afraid of them again.

"Then He gave us His beautiful Torah! Hashem said, 'The Jews are My precious children and I will always love and take care of each and every one of them.'"

Yael's eyes shone. This was a happy story, after all. "But that was a very long time ago, Savta. What does that have to do with Pesach today?"

"It was a very long time ago, sweet girl. But guess what? Hashem still loves us today the same as He loved us then! Every time Pesach comes, we talk about this story. It's like the birthday of Hashem's love for us when He chose us to be special forever! And we remember His Promise to us that very soon He will make many miracles for us again and bring us Mashiach!"

"And that is why we are so excited! When Mommy and I clean and sweep and dust, it's because we are getting ready for the biggest party ever! That party is the Seder!"

"Wow!" said Yael. **"A great big Seder Party sounds so exciting!"**

"Yes! Exactly!" said Savta. "Now are you ready to do a little dance with me?"

Savta clasped Yael's hands in her own and they hopped around in happy little circles.

"Pesach is coming, and we have a lot to do! I'm proud that Hashem loves me. Aren't you proud, too?"

They danced with the vacuum cleaner.

They danced with the broom.

They danced with the mop around the room.

A Savta and Yael Dance!
A Pesach is Coming Dance!
A Happy to be Jewish Dance!

A L'shanah Haba'ah B'Yerushalayim Dance!
Don't you feel like dancing, too?

Here's the Dance for Pesach song!
Won't you sing along?

Clap, clap, clap and clean for Pesach.
Dance, dance, dance and sweep for Pesach.
For this birthday we prepare with love and care.

Sing a song and dust for Pesach.
Hop, hop, hop, and shop for Pesach.
For this birthday we prepare with love and care.

Chorus:
*Pesach is our birthday, for that is when*
*We became special children of Hashem.*
*He freed us from Egypt, He holds us so dear,*
*And the Seder is the grandest party of the year!*

Celebrate with love and pride
The miracles before our eyes —
Ten Makos and split the sea.
He took us out and made us free!

Chorus: *Pesach is our birthday ...*

Hashem made many miracles — so Hashem will again
When Mashiach will arrive, im yirtzeh Hashem!
Just you wait and see how happy the whole world will be
L'shanah Haba'ah, B'Yerushalayim Habenuyah.

Chorus: *Pesach is our birthday ...* 2x

# Also in the LITE Girl Series ...

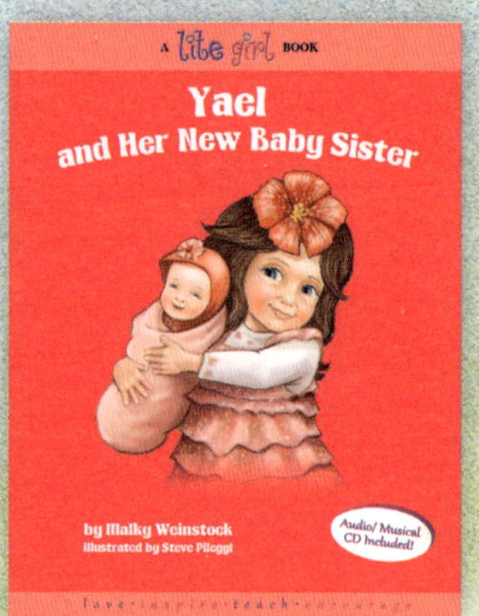

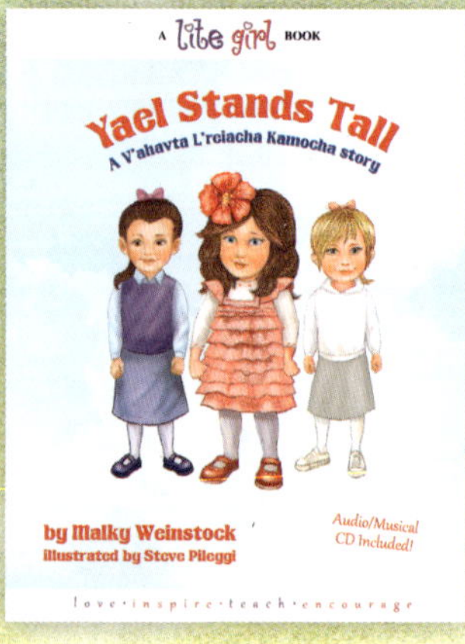

# Also in the Yael Yom Tov Series ...

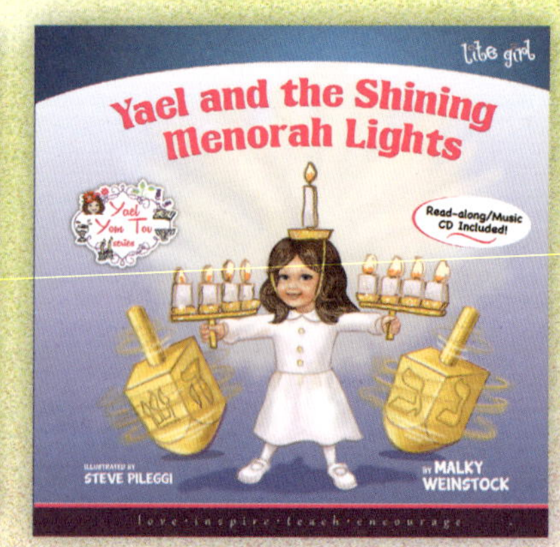